APR 1 5 2003

D1174761

# COLLAPSE!

## The Science of **Structural Engineering Failures**

Structural Engineering Failures...

HEADLINE SCIENCE ...

ctural Engineering Failures ...

by Kirstin Cronn-Mills

Content Adviser:
John Stanton, Ph.D.,
Professor of Structural Engineering and Mechanics,
University of Washington

Science Adviser:
Terrence E. Young Jr., M.Ed., M.L.S.,
Jefferson Parish (Louisiana) Public School System

Reading Adviser:
Rosemary G. Palmer, Ph.D., Department of Literacy,
College of Education, Boise State University

Compass Point Books • 151 Good Counsel Drive, P. O. Box 669 • Mankato, MN 56002-0669

This book was manufactured with paper containing
at least 10 percent post-consumer waste.

**Library of Congress Cataloging-in-Publication Data**
Cronn-Mills, Kirstin, 1968–
 Collapse! : the science of structural engineering failures / by Kirstin Cronn-Mills.
   p. cm.—(Headline Science)
 Includes bibliographical references and index.
 ISBN 978-0-7565-4061-6 (library binding)
 1. Structural failures—Juvenile literature. 2. Structural engineering—Juvenile literature. I. Title.
 TA656.C78 2009
 624.1'71—dc22                                              2008038333

Editor: Anthony Wacholtz
Designers: Ellen Schofield and Ashlee Suker
Page Production: Ashlee Suker
Photo Researcher: Eric Gohl

Art Director: LuAnn Ascheman-Adams
Creative Director: Joe Ewest
Editorial Director: Nick Healy
Managing Editor: Catherine Neitge

Photographs ©: Mandel Ngan/AFP/Getty Images, cover (bottom); DVIC/MCSN Joshua Adam Nuzzo, cover (inset,
left), 34; DVIC/PH1(AW) Brien Aho, USN, cover (inset, middle), 23; June Marie Sobrito/Shutterstock, cover (inset,
right), 19; STR/AFP/Getty Images, 5; James Steidl/Shutterstock, 7; prism_68/Shutterstock, 8; AP Images/The Cana-
dian Press, Jonathan Hayward, 9; YONHAP/AFP/Getty Images, 11; Kyodo via AP Images, 12; Spencer Platt/Getty
Images, 14; AP Images, 15, 25, 29; Jose Jimenez/Primera Hora/Getty Images, 16; Thomas Nilsson/Getty Images, 17;
Bentley Archive/Popperfoto/Getty Images, 18; NASA/Jeff Schmaltz, MODIS Land Rapid Response Team, 21; Jerry
Grayson/Helifilms Australia PTY Ltd/Getty Images, 24; Mario Tama/Getty Images, 26; AFP/Getty Images, 28; AP
Images/Chitose Suzuki, 30; Scott Olson/Getty Images, 32; AP Images/John Weeks III, 33; AP Images/Pete Leabo,
35; Mark Wilson/Getty Images, 36; AP Images/St. Cloud Times, Kimm Anderson, 37; AP Images/Toby Talbot, 39;
Toshifumi Kitamura/AFP/Getty Images, 40; AP Images/Douglas C. Pizac, 41; Uwe Halstenbach/iStockphoto, 42;
Wikipedia, public-domain image, 43.

The author would like to thank Dr. Karen C. Chou, PE, ASCE, and Dr. Aaron S. Budge, ASCE,
for their help with this book.

Visit Compass Point Books on the Internet at *www.compasspointbooks.com*
or e-mail your request to *custserv@compasspointbooks.com*

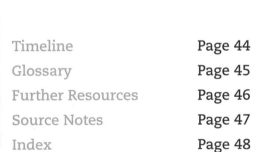

# BUILDING COLLAPSES IN AZERBAIJAN

>>> BBC News
August 29, 2007

A 14-story building under construction in Azerbaijan's capital has collapsed, killing at least five people. Rescue workers have been searching for survivors trapped under tons of rubble since the building fell across a road in Baku on Tuesday.

Emergency services have pulled four people out alive from the wreckage so far, according to Reuters. But a mobile phone call from a man trapped in the basement revealed that at least five others are still alive. The exact number of survivors is unclear, with some reports suggesting that there were 10 people trapped in the basement. ...

Baku city prosecutor Aziz Seidov told reporters that initial evidence pointed to shoddy construction work as the cause of the collapse.

Imagine building a model house on your kitchen table—a house that looks and works just like the house you live in. There are many pieces and parts, and you'd need to make sure everything fit together. You probably wouldn't know how to create all the working parts of the model house yourself, so you would have to get other people to help. If each person does his or her part well, your model house could be a success.

Now imagine what would happen if your model house collapsed. Your house might become a big heap on the table, but it would probably be easy to clean up, and no one would be hurt. But what would happen if a real building collapsed?

*On August 28, 2007, a large crowd gathered around the rubble of a high-rise residential building after it collapsed in Baku, the capital of Azerbaijan.*

**KEEPING CURRENT**

News changes every minute, and readers need access to the latest information to keep current. Here are a few key search terms to help you locate up-to-the-minute structural engineering headlines:

bridge safety

earthquake testing

Federal Emergency
   Management Agency

OSHA structural failure

progressive collapses

structural design failures

United States levees

U.S. Fire Administration
   structural collapse

When an actual building, bridge, or other structure collapses, people can be hurt or killed. People may be trapped under the structure or under falling debris. Rubble from the collapse can cover a large area and cost millions or even billions of dollars to clean up.

What causes these structures to collapse? With your model house, your sister could run by and shake the table, causing your house to fall. On a larger scale, natural forces such as earthquakes can cause structural collapse. Another reason for a structural failure is that the building materials don't hold up. If your model house was built with paper instead of wood or metal, it would probably not last long. The same is true for real structures. For example, if a bridge is built with the wrong type of metal, it may not be able to support many vehicles, and the bridge might collapse.

## STRUCTURAL INTEGRITY

The goal of any structural engineering project is to make sure the parts of a structure work together to keep the structure upright and durable. This is called structural integrity. From skyscrapers to garages, the idea is that all the materials fit together to build the strongest structure possible.

Several people work together to ensure a building's structural integrity. First, an architect draws out the blueprints, or plans. He or she creates the size and layout of the structure based on what is needed or how the building will be used.

Engineers also create plans that go with the architect's blueprints. They decide what materials should be used to make the structure. They also have the most responsibility for making sure everything is built correctly. Engineers working on buildings, bridges, and roads also choose the right material for the structure. Most structures are made of a combination of wood, metal, glass, and concrete.

Once the architects and engineers work out the plans and the materials are selected, a building contractor builds the structure according to the plans. People at the job site include construction workers, engineers, site supervisors, and safety inspectors.

HEADLINE SCIENCE

*A site's superintendent—who leads the building crew—and lead engineer consult the blueprints during construction.*

As the structure is built, these people continue to check on its safety.

Engineers and architects have to consider many questions when they choose the materials and construction methods to be used. For example, how long is the structure intended to last before it becomes out of date and needs to be replaced?

You would probably want a skyscraper to have a longer life than a bus shelter, so you would build it out of better materials and make it stronger. How many people might be hurt if the structure collapsed? A skyscraper collapse would kill many more people than the collapse of a bus shelter, so it makes sense to build the skyscraper with better materials. How harsh is the environment that the structure has to withstand? Bridges carry trucks that cause vibrations, and they have to withstand temperature changes and bad weather. The "skeleton," or structure, of a building is usually protected inside the building's outer materials. That is why it is harder to make a bridge last a long time.

There must also be adequate space available to build a structure. If

*With the number of people needed to build a structure, engineering and architecture are two popular careers in the United States. In 2007, almost 2.5 million people were employed in one of these fields.*

On April 26, 2008, more than 40 people were injured when the floor collapsed during a Christian rock concert at a church in British Columbia. The church's youth pastor said the floor was not meant to hold the hundreds of people who gathered near the stage and danced to the music.

engineers tried to build a structure in a space that was smaller than they had planned, they might not have room to include proper supports. That is why many countries have building laws and regulations in place. Most states in the United States follow the International Code Council's requirements for structural safety. The ICC develops codes for both residential and commercial construction.

## STRUCTURAL FAILURE

Despite the preparation that goes into construction, there are several reasons why structures collapse. One of the most common reasons is that the load was too big. Every structure has a specific amount of weight it can hold. If too much weight is put on a structure, it will collapse.

Think back to your model house. You may decide to put a sofa on the floor of the second-story living room. If the floor isn't strong enough to hold the added weight of the sofa, the floor will collapse. This first collapse might cause walls and more floors to fall.

Load is very important to a building's structural integrity. Any structure must be built to withstand the maximum weight it was designed to carry. But if the maximum weight is exceeded, the building might fall.

Another possible reason behind a structural collapse is that the right materials were not chosen for the job. For your model house, if you used a pile of plastic drinking straws instead of the kitchen table, the house would probably fall before long. In the same sense, the right materials for a construction job are very important. Engineers have to decide what will be the strongest material for the condi-

tions the structure will face. Picking the wrong materials could lead to a structural disaster.

A structure might also fall because the materials are weak or have flaws in them. This would be the case if the wood you used to build your model house had cracks in it. Any weight that was added might cause the wood to snap. In a sports stadium, the roof is often made from a web of steel pieces. If one of them has a crack in it or is not straight, it could fracture or buckle, causing the whole roof to collapse.

The right type of connectors to hold the building materials together is also crucial to a building's integrity. Connectors can be items such as nails, screws, rivets, and metal plates. They are the key to holding together the big pieces of a structure. With the model house, if you use regular glue instead of a wood glue, the second story might fall if any weight is added. There have been several cases where faulty connectors have led to real structural collapses. Often large parts of a structure

*A department store in Seoul, South Korea, collapsed in 1995, killing about 500 people and injuring more than 900. Poor workmanship was cited as the reason for the collapse.*

work on a structure, fatal mistakes can happen. This is one of the main reasons that the West Gate bridge in Melbourne, Australia, collapsed during construction.

The weather is another important factor. For example, a bridge might not last as long in a place where it snows because of the salt used to melt the ice on the bridge. The salt might rust the steel girders of the bridge, and the weight from the traffic might cause the weakened steel to break. Also, hurricanes, earthquakes, and other natural disasters can be devastating to any type of structure.

Sometimes structural failures are caused by a combination of several factors. A structure could have the wrong connectors and weak flooring materials. Or maybe the architect forgot to consult the engineer, and

have to be brought to a building site individually and put together there. If the connectors used to put together those pieces are weak, the connectors break and the structure might fall.

A lack of communication can contribute to any kind of structural failure as well. For example, if the engineers and architects don't talk to each other while they make the plans, the walls of the structure might not be built in the right way or with the right materials. If communication doesn't happen among all the people who

*A 7.9-magnitude earthquake destroyed thousands of buildings in southwestern China in May 2008. The earthquake claimed the lives of almost 70,000 people.*

the bolts used were the wrong size. If more than one thing is wrong with a structure, a "domino effect" may occur. For example, an older building could be strong enough to withstand normal loads from wind and the weight of the people inside, but it might collapse during an earthquake. If either the building had been stronger or the earthquake had not occurred, the building would have remained standing. ◤

# A DAY OF TERROR

*The New York Times*
September 12, 2001

The cause of the twin collapse yesterday of the World Trade Center towers in downtown Manhattan was most likely the intense fire fed by thousands of gallons of jet fuel aboard the two jetliners that crashed into the buildings, experts on skyscraper design said.

The high temperatures, of perhaps 1,000 to 2,000 degrees, probably weakened the steel supports, the experts said, causing the external walls to buckle and allowing the floors above to fall almost straight down. That led to catastrophic failures of the rest of the buildings.

The towers were built to withstand the stresses of hurricane-force winds and to survive the heat of ordinary fires.

On the morning of September 11, 2001, the World Trade Center towers in lower Manhattan crashed to the ground. Each building was 110 stories high, and each had been hit by a Boeing 767 taken over by terrorists. More than 2,700 people died as a result of the collapse, and more than 6,000 people were injured. The North Tower was hit first, and it fell 102 minutes after the crash. After the South Tower was hit, it stood for 56 minutes before it collapsed.

The project engineers had chosen a new way to build the Twin Towers in the 1960s. Before that time, most buildings were built with an interlocking system of steel beams that looked like grid paper. Leslie Robertson, the chief engineer, designed the Twin Towers to have a framework of hollow tubes of steel in their outside walls. The engineers chose to use hollow steel core sides for the buildings because of the danger of strong winds. Imagine pointing a hair dryer set on "high" at your model house. That would be about the same effect as the wind at the top of high skyscrapers.

In the center of each building was the elevator core—a strong

The two airliners that crashed into the Twin Towers were hijacked by terrorists.

rectangular steel tower. The core provided strength to the whole building and contained the elevator and stairs. Offices filled up the space between the core and the outside walls. The floors of the offices were supported on steel trusses—skeletal beams that support the floor or roof—that stretched between the core and the outside walls.

The engineers knew it was possible for skyscrapers to be hit by airplanes. They built the towers to withstand the force of a Boeing 707, the biggest jet made at that time. Knowing that a jet collision would cause an enormous fire, the engineers also had fireproofing material applied to the steel while the buildings were being constructed. Fireproof drywall material covered the steel core as well.

*More than 200,000 tons (180,000 metric tons) of structural steel was used in the construction of the Twin Towers.*

## WHY THE TWIN TOWERS COLLAPSED

The first jet hit the North Tower between the 93rd and 98th floors and destroyed the center core of the building. The second jet hit the South Tower, taking out a corner of the building between the 78th and 84th floors. The jet fuel began to burn immediately in both buildings. The fuel burned off quickly, but it set office furniture and other interior materials on fire. The

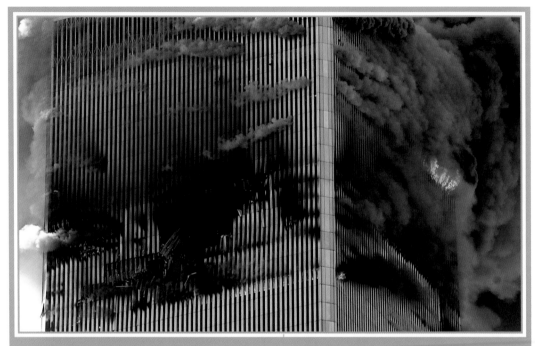

*The fires started by the jets' fuel after the impacts weakened the buildings' materials and were a major reason the towers collapsed.*

forces of the jets and the fires greatly reduced the strength of the buildings.

After the impacts, the hollow steel core walls of each building held the load that the missing sides of the building were supposed to carry. However, when the jets hit the buildings, the impact blew off the fireproofing material the engineers had applied to the steel during construction. The burning jet fuel set the offices on fire, and those fires further weakened the walls and floors.

If the jet fuel had burned out without starting any other fires, the structures might have remained standing because the steel would not have melted. But the fire from the burning offices caused the floor trusses to melt and sag. During construction, the trusses were bolted to the steel core and then welded to the steel tubes in the outside walls. When the trusses began to melt, they couldn't support the weight of the office floors. As the floors began to sag, they pulled the outside walls inward and bent until they finally broke.

What happened to the Twin Towers is called a progressive collapse—where one floor falls onto another floor. The South Tower collapsed from the outside walls to the inside core. The collapse most likely happened because there were more than 20 floors to support above the hole in the building's side. The rest of the building couldn't hold the weight.

*The top floors of the South Tower fell away from the point of the jet's impact. They collapsed in the direction of the floors that were on fire.*

The North Tower fell straight down. Its floors "pancaked" down on top of each other. It looked like a demolition, when construction crews blow up a building on purpose. Even though the North Tower had fewer floors to support above the hole in its side, its center core had been badly damaged. What was left of the core could not support the building's weight once the steel began to melt.

## AFTER 9/11

Engineers studied the wreckage from the Twin Towers after the pieces were placed in salvage yards in New Jersey. They could see how the steel warped

### NOW YOU KNOW

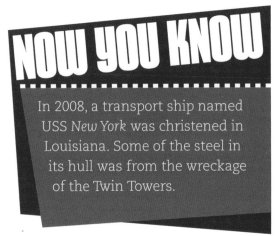

In 2008, a transport ship named USS *New York* was christened in Louisiana. Some of the steel in its hull was from the wreckage of the Twin Towers.

### < RONAN POINT >

In 1968, an apartment building in a London suburb collapsed, killing four people. The building—Ronan Point—collapsed because a gas explosion knocked out a wall on the 18th floor. That wall had helped hold up the four floors above it because it was a load-bearing wall. After the explosion, the southeast corner of the apartment building collapsed like a house of cards—once the one wall was removed, the rest of the walls tumbled inward.

from the heat because they could track where some of the steel beams had been. Some beams had numbers engraved on them to indicate which floors they came from. The engineers also studied the trusses connecting the elevator core to the outside walls. They determined that the trusses gave way in the fire.

The Twin Towers weren't the only buildings that failed that day. The World Trade Center complex had seven buildings in it. Three of them, including the Twin Towers, collapsed when the jets hit. Another building was crushed by debris from the towers. These buildings were damaged beyond repair and were demolished. The debris from the towers also destroyed a church and a bank. The collapse of the World Trade Center towers and the destruction of the other buildings in the complex made it the largest structural failure in U.S. history.

*Every year on September 11, two beacons light the sky in memory of those who died in the terrorist attacks.*

# EXPERTS SAY FAULTY LEVEES CAUSED MUCH OF FLOODING

*The Washington Post*
September 21, 2005

[W]ith the help of complex computer models and stark visual evidence, scientists and engineers at Louisiana State University's Hurricane Center have concluded that Katrina's surges did not come close to overtopping those barriers (flood walls). That would make faulty design, inadequate construction or some combination of the two the likely cause of the breaching of the floodwalls along the 17th Street and London Avenue canals—and the flooding of most of New Orleans. ...

But Ivor van Herdeen, the Hurricane Center's deputy director, said the real scandal of Katrina is the "catastrophic structural failure" of barriers that should have handled the hurricane with relative ease.

Hurricane Katrina hit the northeast Gulf Coast of the United States on August 29, 2005. The storm caused damage in Louisiana, Mississippi, and Alabama. It was the third strongest hurricane ever to reach land in the United States. The storm caused more than $81 billion in damage, making it the most expensive natural disaster in U.S. history.

*Less than a day before Hurricane Katrina hit Louisiana, satellite images from NASA showed the enormous area covered by the storm.*

Hurricane Katrina created a flood in New Orleans, Louisiana. Almost 80 percent of the city was under water for several days. About 1,500 people died in and around New Orleans because of the flood. Then the city flooded again when Hurricane Rita hit Louisiana and Texas less than a month later. The floods destroyed thousands of houses and other structures. Some buildings were picked up and carried by the force of the water. At some points in the city, the floodwater was 20 feet (6 meters) deep.

While most cities are built on dry, firm ground, New Orleans was built on wet, spongy land. Much of the city is lower than the rest of the land and water around it. The homes in New Orleans have no basements because the water level is so high. Every day water is pumped out from beneath the city so it doesn't seep up from the ground.

Because the city sits in the ground instead of on the ground, it must rely on levees, or flood walls, to keep out lake and river water. A levee is built anywhere land needs to be protected from water. Levees can be made of earth, building materials, or a combination of both. Some levees occur naturally from a buildup of silt or sand pushed out of a river or lake by the waves. The levees in New Orleans were human-made. The first ones were built in 1718, around the time the city was built. They were only 3 feet (90 centimeters) high. Today there are 200 miles (320 kilometers) of levees around New Orleans.

## HURRICANE KATRINA

As Hurricane Katrina hit New Orleans, the force of the storm churned up the bodies of water around the city. Then the city was flooded with water from Lake Pontchartrain, the Mississippi River, and city canals. In some places the water washed over the levees. This process is called overtopping. Levees also flooded because some of the water pushed hard enough to burst the levees open. Levees breached in about 50 spots around the city.

The levees in New Orleans failed because of their poor design. Some of the anchor posts (also called pilings) for the levees were not put into the ground deeply enough to hold up the levee walls. Some of the anchor posts, which usually are made of steel, were not as strong and thick as they needed to be. The levees varied in quality and structure because they were built at various times in various ways. Some levees may have needed major maintenance, which also could have contributed to their failure.

The soil was also a problem. Some posts were in the peat layer of the soil. Peat is a spongy, soft soil found in swamps, and it does not support construction very well. When the

*National Guard soldiers surveyed the flooded streets of New Orleans from helicopters and then landed to assist the victims of Hurricane Katrina.*

*Sandbags were dropped from a military helicopter to fill a gap in one of the levees two weeks after Katrina hit.*

force of the water pushed the levees, the support posts gave way because the peat could not hold the posts steady. Soil over some of the levees had also been washed away over the years, making it easier for water to get through them. Some levees may have been built with poor concrete, and water may have gotten through levees that were incomplete. Many of the levee breaches happened where levee or wall sections joined together. These spots are weaker than solid levee walls.

# Chapter 3: *A Deadly Design*

Some scientists say New Orleans is gradually sinking lower into the swamps on which it is built. Sinking ground may have also affected how the levees worked during Hurricane Katrina. The settling ground may have pulled away from the levee walls to make them less stable. The ground may have sunk almost 3 feet (90 cm) since some of the levees were built.

## AFTER KATRINA

Civil engineers and other experts conducted five investigations after New Orleans flooded. The engineers determined three reasons for the levee breaches. Some of the levees were overtopped. Others were pushed open. Some were pulled out of the ground because of lack of support from the soil. All five studies agreed that the levee breaches, not the hurricane itself, caused the flooding in New Orleans.

According to an American Society of Civil Engineers report released in 2007, the risk of New Orleans flooding was more than 1,000 times greater than cit-

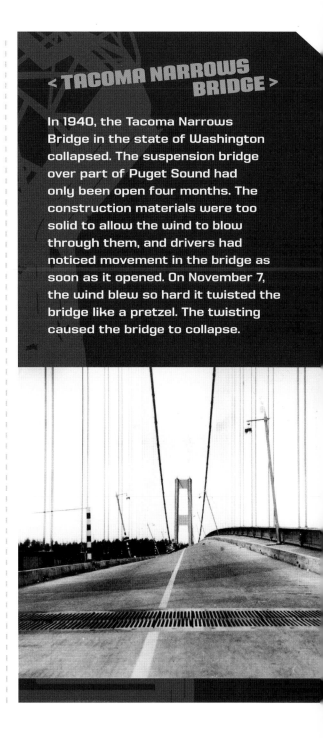

**< TACOMA NARROWS BRIDGE >**

In 1940, the Tacoma Narrows Bridge in the state of Washington collapsed. The suspension bridge over part of Puget Sound had only been open four months. The construction materials were too solid to allow the wind to blow through them, and drivers had noticed movement in the bridge as soon as it opened. On November 7, the wind blew so hard it twisted the bridge like a pretzel. The twisting caused the bridge to collapse.

*After the water levels receded following Hurricane Katrina, workers raced to finish repairs on the New Orleans levees before the start of the next hurricane season.*

ies built behind any dam in the United States. This report called the levee breaches in New Orleans "the worst engineering catastrophe in U.S. history."

Engineers are studying ways to build better levees in New Orleans. One suggestion is to use T-shaped steel beams instead of I-shaped ones. The T-beams would be placed so the soil covers the top of the T, giving three directions of support to the levees. Engineers will continue to discover new ways to fix the levees as they study what happened. Engineers also have much better tools to design levees than when the original levees were built in 1965. The engineers who are studying the levees also hope to create levee design regulations that are more like those for dams, which are much stronger. No matter how engineers decide to fix the levees, it will cost many billions of dollars to build new ones.

# MORE BODIES RECOVERED IN VIETNAM BRIDGE COLLAPSE

*USA Today*
September 27, 2007

Workers continued searching for bodies Thursday after a section of a massive bridge under construction in southern Vietnam collapsed. ...

"We were working normally and all of a sudden we were flying down," [Nguyen Quoc] Trung said.

He landed semiconscious, with his chest stuck between concrete and twisted metal.

"I didn't know if I was in the jungle or the middle of the air," Trung said. "I didn't know where I was."

On September 26, 2007, an unfinished bridge collapsed in southern Vietnam. The bridge was being built over the Hau (Bassac) River near the city of Can Tho. It was intended to carry four lanes of traffic. The break happened in a long section of an approach ramp, which was more than 98 feet (30 m) above the ground. About 50 people were killed, and more than 150 people were injured.

There are many possible reasons why the Can Tho bridge collapsed. Rain may have softened the foundations of the bridge or the soil around them. Some scaffolding (supports) could have been removed too early from beneath newly poured concrete

*Rescue workers used a crane to search for people trapped in the rubble of the Can Tho bridge.*

HEADLINE
SCIENCE

*Many workers at the site assisted rescue crews in transporting the injured to hospitals.*

bridge decks. The scaffolding may have been too weak to support the weight of the concrete. The scaffolding could have sunk into the ground instead of standing firm. Sinking would change how much weight the scaffolding could support. Landslides near the scaffolding may also have caused the supports to shift.

## FOLLOWING THE COLLAPSE

The Vietnamese Ministries of Transport and Public Security formed a team to study the site. These inspectors believe some of the external pressures came from human error. Most errors related to the scaffolding.

About nine months before the collapse, a Japanese construction company had recommended that a higher load

# NOW YOU KNOW

On March 27, 1981, the Harbor Cay Condominium collapsed in Cocoa Beach, Florida. One of the main reasons for the failure was because frost prevented the concrete from gaining strength. One floor collapsed as a result, which triggered a progressive collapse. Eleven people were killed, and 27 were injured.

capacity was needed for supports of the new bridge pilings—the columns underneath the bridge that support the bridge's weight. The consultant asked the building crews to use international standards to determine the appropriate safety measures. No one is certain whether safety inspections took place at the Can Tho bridge. In October 2007, the Ministry of Public Security of Vietnam took legal action against the contractors who removed the scaffolding before the concrete was hardened.

*Construction resumed on a bridge between Can Tho and Vinh Long Province in August 2008 after a new support system was designed and approved.*

# DESIGN FLAW CALLED CRITICAL FACTOR IN MINN. BRIDGE COLLAPSE

>>> *USA Today*
January 15, 2008

The Interstate 35W bridge in Minneapolis was built with steel connectors that were half as thick as they should have been, "the critical factor" in the August collapse that killed 13 and injured 144, the National Transportation Safety Board announced today.

The connectors, known as gusset plates, tie steel girders together. They should have been an inch thick but were only a half-inch, said NTSB Chairman Mark Rosenker. He called that "the critical factor" resulting from an "error in calculation" by the designers. But he said the agency has not yet determined the "probable cause" of the collapse.

On August 1, 2007, the I-35W bridge fell during evening rush-hour traffic in Minneapolis, Minnesota. The bridge spanned the Mississippi River and was part of northbound Interstate 35-West. When the bridge fell, rescuers used disaster techniques developed after the Twin Towers fell to save as many people as possible. At least 50 vehicles fell into the Mississippi River, along with debris from the bridge. Thirteen people died and 144 were injured in the collapse.

The bridge carried eight lanes of traffic, four moving north and four moving south. When the bridge collapsed, some of the lanes were closed for construction, so it was carrying

## NOW YOU KNOW

The official name of the I-35W bridge is the St. Anthony Falls Bridge. It was named after the only major natural waterfall on the upper Mississippi River.

*Several vehichles remained on the bridge after the 60-foot (18.3-m) fall.*

fewer cars than normal. But road construction vehicles and equipment were on site. The bridge was important to traffic flowing into and out of the cities of Minneapolis and St. Paul.

The bridge was more than 1,900 feet (580 m) long. Construction started in 1964, and the bridge was opened to traffic in 1967. It was a truss arch bridge, which means steel members formed an arch to connect the steel beams under the bridge deck. The arches were used to support the weight of the bridge deck as it crossed over the river.

The bridge had been inspected and maintained regularly since it was built, but many inspectors had noticed

*The truss arch design of the I-35W bridge may have been one of the reasons behind the collapse.*

the structure's life span was nearing its end. Cracks had been noted several times during inspections.

## WHY THE I-35W BRIDGE COLLAPSED

Engineers and inspectors of the I-35W bridge have focused their investigation on the gusset plates that held the trusses together. A gusset plate is a metal plate used to connect steel pieces in a truss. Most experts agree the bridge collapsed because its gusset plates weren't strong enough.

Inspectors have also focused on how the gusset plates were attached to the beams. The bridge's gusset plates were riveted to the steel mem-

*A mobile diving and salvage unit assessed the wreckage before sending U.S. Navy divers into the river to pull out debris and search for victims.*

bers. Rivets were used to connect steel pieces until the 1960s, but high-strength bolts are now used instead.

## < WALKWAY DISASTER >

On July 17, 1981, two walkways collapsed in the lobby of the Hyatt Regency Crown Center Hotel in Kansas City, Missouri. The walkways were suspended over the lobby. More than 2,000 people had gathered to watch a dance contest. The walkways collapsed because the connectors couldn't hold the load of all the people. The collapse killed 114 people, and more than 200 were injured.

The bolts are stronger and do not work loose in the same way rivets sometimes do.

When the bridge was designed and constructed in the 1960s, engineers did not accurately predict how much extra traffic it would carry as time went on. Engineers also could not predict the increased weight of cars and trucks crossing the bridge.

In addition, construction work was being done on the bridge deck when it collapsed. The construction equipment and sand for the project added about 300 tons (270 metric tons) of weight to the deck. The extra weight may have contributed to the collapse. Some engineers claim this extra weight was about the same as the weight of cars that would have been traveling over the bridge if all the lanes had been open. Other engineers think the weight of the vehicles wouldn't have come close to the added weight of the sand and construction equipment.

Other factors may have affected the connectors. The salt used to de-ice the bridge in the winter played a role in rusting the steel under the bridge. The bridge was designed without a backup system, so if one member or connection failed, the whole bridge would collapse. Any of these factors could have contributed to the bridge's collapse. Today construction designs include a backup system in case part of the structure fails.

## AFTER THE COLLAPSE

Soon after the bridge collapsed, many other bridges in Minnesota were inspected. Once the gusset plates were suspected as the cause of the I-35W bridge collapse, all bridges with those types of gusset plates were re-inspected. Because of these inspections, the DeSoto Bridge in St. Cloud, Minnesota, was

*Members of the National Transportation Safety Board examined the fallen section of the I-35W bridge for clues as to why the bridge collapsed.*

HEADLINE
SCIENCE

Crewmen from the Minnesota Department of Transportation checked the girders underneath the DeSoto Bridge two days after the I-35W bridge collapsed.

closed to traffic in March 2008. Like the I-35W bridge, the DeSoto Bridge is a steel truss. Another bridge in Winona, Minnesota, was closed for repairs in June 2008.

A replacement bridge has been built where the original I-35W bridge collapsed. It cost about $234 million and opened in September 2008. The bridge was built to last 100 years and is made of concrete instead of steel. It is 189 feet (57.6 m) wide, which is about 80 feet (24.4 m) wider than the old bridge.

# NEW I-35W BRIDGE HAS SMART BRIDGE TECHNOLOGY

*The Seattle Times*
September 17, 2008

A stream of data will be flowing from hundreds of sensors in the new Interstate 35W bridge Thursday morning when commuters drive across it for the first time since the old bridge collapsed into the Mississippi River 13 months ago.

The purpose of the "smart bridge" technology isn't to warn of another impending disaster, it's to detect small problems before they become big ones, said Alan Phipps, design manager for the project with Figg Engineering Group Inc. of Tallahassee, Fla.

"What these sensors are for, it's like going to your doctor for your health checkup," Phipps said. "It's to ensure you're maintained in top shape so you never get close to having a serious problem."

Think back to the model house on your kitchen table. If it fell down, you would be able to study it to find the flaws in its construction. Once you knew where the problems were, you could build a stronger house. Scientists do the same thing when a large structure collapses. Any structural failure provides a chance to make improvements that may prevent collapses in the future.

Monitors are one way to keep structures in good shape. The new I-35W bridge in Minneapolis has 323 sensors in its design. Some sensors track how the concrete bridge deck is reacting to traffic, and some follow how the weather affects the bridge. Other sensors monitor how the bridge expands and contracts in various seasons. The data are transmitted on a wireless signal to a control room full

*Steven Arms, president of MicroStrain Inc., displayed an experimental solar-powered device with wireless sensors that could help monitor the status of bridges.*

of computers. The information they provide allows engineers to act if they see something start to go wrong.

Another way to keep structures healthy is to control the vibrations that affect them. Imagine what would happen to your model house if 10 of your friends came running through the kitchen at the same time. The vibrations generated by your friends' movements could knock down your house. Engineers and scientists use many methods to control the vibrations that shake structures. These methods are especially important in areas of the world where earthquakes or strong storms occur.

Some of the most damaging forces

*Shake tables are often used to test structural designs. A model structure is placed on the shake table, which engineers use to simulate the effects of an earthquake.*

## Chapter 6: *Better Building*

In 2003, steel and rubber supports meant to absorb movement and vibrations were placed below a government building in Salt Lake City, Utah.

to act on structures are caused by the ground shaking during an earthquake. While it would be possible to protect structures from earthquake damage just by making them extremely strong, they would be expensive, and most people could not afford to build them.

Instead, engineers have developed ways of protecting structures from the worst effects of these shaking forces.

One way is to use "seismic isolation." The idea is to prevent the ground from shaking the structure. Most of the shaking of an earthquake is horizontal.

Engineers came up with a design to separate the structure from the ground by placing the structure on a very slippery surface. When the ground shakes, the structure remains still while the ground moves underneath it. To prevent the structure from sliding when the wind blows, engineers added a spring to bring it back to where it started once the earthquake stops. Other seismic isolation systems use flexible rubber mountings instead of slippery surfaces to reduce the the structure's movement when the ground shakes.

Another way of protecting a structure is to allow it to bend without breaking. Imagine taking some wooden building blocks with holes through them and lining them

*Taipei 101, one of the world's tallest buildings, stands 1,671 feet (509 m) high.*

# Chapter 6: *Better Building*

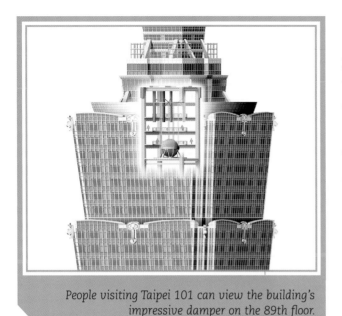

*People visiting Taipei 101 can view the building's impressive damper on the 89th floor.*

Tall skyscrapers need protection from wind vibrations, especially on their highest floors. Taipei 101, a skyscraper in Taipei, Taiwan, has a damper—a type of shock absorber—that is suspended between the 87th and 91st floors. The damper absorbs energy from the building's walls as they move. The walls are attached to the damper by hydraulic cylinders, similar to the ones that pull screen doors shut in houses. When the top floors of the skyscraper shake, the vibration is transferred from the walls to the damper through the cylinders. The damper absorbs the vibrations and prevents the walls from shaking too much.

Engineers and scientists continue to consider new ideas for safer structures. With each collapse, new methods are developed to construct more secure buildings and bridges. Engineers hope that these new developments will lead to fewer structural failures. ◼

up in a row. Then feed a rubber band through the holes, stretching it tight and tying it at each end. The rubber band would clamp the blocks together so they form a wooden beam. You could bend the beam, but when you let go, the rubber band would snap the beam back to its original shape. Engineers have started to use this idea in structures. Instead of small wooden blocks, they use chunks of concrete. Instead of rubber bands, they use strong steel cables to connect the blocks of concrete.

**27th century B.C.**
Imhotep, the first engineer known by name, builds the first step pyramid in Egypt

**26th century B.C.**
The Great Pyramid of Giza is constructed; the pyramid was one of the seven wonders of the ancient world

**1847**
The Dee Bridge in England collapses as a train passes over it; five people are killed

**1879**
The 3-mile (4.8-km) cast-iron Tay Rail Bridge in Scotland falls as a train passes over it during a storm, killing 75 people; most bridges are constructed of steel after this time

**1887–1889**
The Eiffel Tower is built with iron in Paris, even though steel is being used throughout the world for building construction

**1950s–1960s**
Fazlur Khan designs many new structural systems to reinforce buildings; his designs are incorporated into the John Hancock Center and Sears Tower in Chicago

**1968**
Ronan Point, a 22-story apartment building in London, collapses because of a gas explosion on the 18th floor; four people are killed

**1981**
Two suspended walkways collapse in the Hyatt Regency Hotel in Kansas City, Missouri, killing 114 people; the Harbor Cay Condominium collapses in Cocoa Beach, Florida, and 11 workers are killed

**1993**
One block of the Highland Towers apartments collapses in Kuala Lumpur, Malaysia, killing 48

**2001**
The Twin Towers of the World Trade Center collapse after hijacked jets hit the buildings; more than 2,700 people are killed

**2005**
The levees that protect New Orleans are destroyed by the forces of Hurricane Katrina, and 80 percent of the city is flooded; about 1,500 people are killed

**2007**
The I-35W bridge spanning the Mississippi River in Minneapolis, Minnesota, collapses during rush-hour traffic; 13 people are killed

**2009**
Construction on the world's tallest skyscraper, Burj Dubai, is set for completion in Dubai City, United Arab Emirates; the skyscraper will have at least 160 stories and be more than 2,600 feet (800 m) tall

Timeline

# GLOSSARY

**blueprints**
detailed plans of a structure

**breach**
to make an opening or a gap in a structure

**bridge deck**
surface of a bridge where vehicles
are driven

**civil engineer**
person who works on the design,
construction, or maintenance of
any structure

**compromise**
to weaken or damage the strength
of a structure, exposing it to risk

**connectors**
building materials such as nails
and rivets that hold the pieces of
a structure together

**demolition**
blowing up or taking down a structure
on purpose

**gusset plates**
steel plates used to connect two or more
structure members

**levee**
embankment built to prevent a body
of water from overflowing

**life span**
length of time a structure can safely
support a load

**load**
total force or weight that a structure is
designed to withstand or hold

**overtopping**
flow of water over a dam or levee

**pilings**
columns that are drilled or driven into
the earth to carry loads from a structure
down to a stronger layer of soil

**progressive collapse**
when one section of a structure fails to
hold its load and causes other parts of
the structure to fail

**scaffolding**
temporary framework or set of platforms
used to support workers and materials

**shake table**
device used by engineers to simulate the
effect of earthquakes on model structures

**structural engineer**
engineer who designs systems and
structures that support various kinds
of loads

**structural integrity**
all the parts of a structure working
together to keep the structure standing

**trusses**
framework of metal or wooden beams
used to support other materials

# FURTHER RESOURCES

For more information on this topic, use FactHound.

1.  Go to *www.facthound.com*
2.  Choose your grade level.
3.  Begin your search.

This book's ID number is 9780756540616

FactHound will find the best sites for you.

## FURTHER READING

Caney, Steven. *Steven Caney's Ultimate Building Book.*
Philadelphia: Running Press Kids, 2006.

Englar, Mary. *September 11.* Minneapolis: Compass Point
Books, 2007.

Landau, Elaine. *Bridges.* New York: Children's Press, 2001.

Rodger, Ellen. *Hurricane Katrina.* New York: Crabtree Publishing
Company, 2007.

## LOOK FOR OTHER BOOKS IN THIS SERIES:

*Climate Crisis: The Science of
Global Warming*

*Cure Quest: The Science of Stem
Cell Research*

*Feel the G's: The Science of Gravity
and G-Forces*

*Goodbye, Gasoline: The Science of
Fuel Cells*

*Great Shakes: The Science of Earthquakes*

*Orbiting Eyes: The Science of Artificial
Satellites*

*Out of Control: The Science of Wildfires*

*Rise of the Thinking Machines: The Science
of Robots*

*Storm Surge: The Science of Hurricanes*

Chapter 1: "Building Collapses in Azerbaijan." BBC News. 29 Aug. 2007. 7 Oct. 2008. http://news.bbc.co.uk/2/hi/europe/6968624.stm

Chapter 2: James Glanz. "A Day of Terror." *The New York Times.* 12 Sept. 2001. 2 Feb. 2008. http://query.nytimes.com/gst/fullpage.html?res=9B0D E4DD1238F931A2575ACOA9679C8B63&sec=&spon=&pagewanted=print

Chapter 3: Michael Grunwald and Susan B. Glasser. "Experts Say Faulty Levees Caused Much of Flooding." *The Washington Post.* 21 Sept. 2005. 10 March 2008. www.washingtonpost.com/wp-dyn/content/article/ 2005/09/20/AR2005092001894_pf.html

Chapter 4: "More Bodies Recovered in Vietnam Bridge Collapse." *USA Today.* 27 Sept. 2007. 15 Oct. 2008. www.usatoday.com/news/world/2007-09-26-vietnam-bridge_N.htm

Chapter 5: "Design Flaw Called 'Critical Factor' in Minn. Bridge Collapse." *USA Today.* 15 Jan. 2008. 7 Oct. 2008. http://blogs.usatoday.com/ ondeadline/2008/01/faulty-steel-ti.html

Chapter 6: Steve Karnowski. "New I-35W Bridge Has 'Smart Bridge' Technology." *The Seattle Times.* 17 Sept. 2008. 25 Sept. 2008. http://seattletimes.nwsource.com/html/localnews/2008186392_ apmnbridgecollapse.html

# ABOUT THE AUTHOR

Kirstin Cronn-Mills holds a doctorate in rhetoric and professional communication. She teaches English and humanities at South Central College in North Mankato, Minnesota.

# INDEX